To Russ,

Thank you for your interest in my book. Hope you enjoy reading it.

Pete Cla____

Reports of Mass Deception

Exposing the Rhetoric
Regarding the War on Iraq

Peter Chase

Wasteland Press
Louisville, KY USA
www.wastelandpress.com

Reports of Mass Deception:
Exposing the Rhetoric
Regarding the War on Iraq
By Peter Chase

Front Cover Photo by Jack Gordon
Courtesy of the 99th RRC, USAR
First Printing – December, 2003

ISBN: 0-9746290-9-X

Printed in the U.S.A.

For Mario Russell Chase

Acknowledgments

I would never be able to accomplish anything in my professional career without the love and support of my beautiful wife, Brigid Ann Chase. Her unselfish love and devotion to me and our three most awesome children–Brigid Ann Chase, II, Hope Ellen Chase, and Elizabeth Alexandra Chase–make my life the greatest joy any man could ever hope for.

Also, many thanks to my family and friends who have given me much needed advice and encouragement regarding this work. Among them are my father Louis W. Chase, my mother Marie P. Castagna, Phil Castagna, Jimmy Skeels, Lucy Skeels, Bishop George R. Beninate, Pastor Susan S. Beninate, Tara Kennedy, Jeff Kennedy, Randy Gran, Tom Gallant, and Jeff Henzler.

Very special thanks to the editorial staff of the *Monthly Post*, whose undying devotion to the editing of this book went above and beyond the call of duty. They are Karen Knapp, Debbie Smith, and Mary Ann Sarafin.

I would also like to extend a very special thanks to Jack Gordon who was gracious enough to allow me the use of his picture for the cover of this book, and Timothy Veeley of Wasteland Press who gave me the opportunity to have this published by his company.

Last, but certainly foremost, I would like to thank my God, Jesus Christ, whose lordship and love transformed my life from the darkness of emptiness into the light of His resurrection.

Contents

FORWARD

by Jeffrey R. Henzler

Like a Trojan Horse, the United States has long been invaded by forces that seek to divide and conquer. At first, masked by the many familiar faces and voices we all invited into our living rooms, the subtle bias of a leftward leaning media, relentlessly and consistently chiseled away at the foundations of our society and created division using doubt and innuendo. Via the nightly news, our local newspaper or the continual lineup of questionable sitcoms, the extreme left has sought to challenge the foundational values of our American society. Over the past 40 years, the erosion of our culture–politically, educationally, spiritually and familiarly–have stolen away many of our freedoms as we have allowed the mass media complete and unaccountable access into our lives. If left unchecked, within 10 years, we will likely not even recognize the society that we have become.

Over the past 10 years, through the venues of radio, cable, and the internet, the winds of truth have been infiltrating the minds and spirits of millions of Americans, awaking them to what they were once blinded to. The stronghold of liberalism is beginning to dismantle as the socialistic agenda surrounding it are exposed. In each and every area of our culture, the light of truth is being unveiled. Everyday, new books are published, articles are written and television journalists are discovering, researching, and exposing the insidious inaccuracies that are burdening our economy, confusing our children, and distorting the truth about who we are, and where we have come from.

Now, as we are faced with our nation's most difficult battle (terrorism), the truth about Iraq is systematically being stolen away from us everyday as the mainstream news media misreports and distorts the truth about our success in one of history's most providential conflicts.

Reports of Mass Deception: Exposing the Rhetoric Regarding the War on Iraq by Peter Chase unlocks the truth as it challenges, provokes and unravels the myths and falsehoods of our current conflict. The value in Mr. Chase's book is in the facts and research which shed light on the many disregarded parts of truths, not given equal coverage to their more overexposed counterparts. *Reports of Mass Deception* equips you with the knowledge that will allow you to better assess what is the truth regarding the progress with the War on Iraq.

Reports of Mass Deception

CHAPTER 1
The Shroud of Illusion

Reports of Mass Deception

In current times, we hear the bickering of both liberals and conservatives regarding the one side supposedly getting more air time than the other. The liberals argue that the right-wing has more rating-dominant voices that support their position, such as Rush Limbaugh on radio and Bill O'Reilly on television. Conservatives believe that, besides *FOX News Channel* and the exception of a few major newspapers, the mainstream news media is liberally biased. In both cases, they are right, according to Americans.

In the most recent poll conducted by the Gallup Organization regarding America's perception of the news media, 45% of Americans opine that the mainstream news media in the United States are liberally slanted, while only 14% say they're too conservative. According to Gallup, this perception of liberal propensity has not changed over the last few years. Most Americans, who describe their political views as conservative, observe liberal leanings in the news media, while approximately a third of liberals perceive a conservative bias in the news media.[1]

The *Rush Limbaugh Show* attracts nearly 20 million listeners in more than 650 radio markets, worldwide. The *O'Reilly Factor*, with Bill O'Reilly, who is not a conservative but more of an independent, is now the most watched daily prime time cable news program in the country, according to rating statistics by Nielsen Media

Research. Considering these facts, the left's argument is understandable. However, just because these few entities are getting such high-ranking viewer numbers, doesn't mean that the majority of mainstream media news outlets holds a conservative, right-wing view. They get high ratings because they expose the news items that most Americans espouse.

A recent survey conducted by the National Survey of the Role of Polls in Policymaking sheds light on the percentages of liberal dominance in the media industry and policy making field. 4% of 1,206 surveyed identified themselves as Republican. Only 6% said they identify themselves as conservative. The survey included 301 media professionals comprising reporters and editors from top news organizations, and TV and radio networks.[2]

Homogeneous with that survey is another poll that was conducted by *Editor and Publisher* magazine in January 1998, surveying 167 newspaper editors across the country. The poll showed that 89% thought that the public viewed newspapers as liberal compared to 1.2% who thought they were conservatively biased. The same survey posed a question of how often they felt a journalist's bias would influence a story's coverage. 14% said often, while 57% said sometimes. Collectively, that is 71% who acknowledged a bias trend in newspaper coverage.[3]

It is obvious to many Americans that the mainstream

news media are predominantly liberally biased in their coverage, an observation scientifically noted by the Gallup Organization. In fact, if you're a conservative and watch the mainstream news on networks other than the *FOX News Channel*, you may think your conservative leanings are within the minority in America. That is why networks like the *FOX News Channel* receive such high ratings. Viewers are starting to awaken and see that there are a few faces in the mainstream news media who actually agree with their points of view.

In general, the news media would lead you to presuppose that everyone agrees with the Hollywood left's assessment of the Bush administration, which is the misconception that most Americans consider President Bush's performance in the Oval Office a failure thus far. They would lead you to deem that a larger majority of Americans think that saying the Pledge of Allegiance is no longer appropriate. The news media conveys an illusion depicting a vast majority of Americans who are pro-choice and not in favor of prayer in schools or during sporting events such as NASCAR. In fact, a naive, uninformed channel surfer, stumbling upon a news debate, might get the sense that George W. Bush has similar traits to Darth Vader, needlessly pressing for war, thus putting the nation's economy and homeland security in greater risk. By and large, the mainstream news media deceives the American public into a false sense of populace position. This is done with resounding overexposed news coverage of partial portions of the truth, not merely to boost interest by generating needless controversy, but to brainwash the majority into believing they are the minority.

This strategy of hearsay manipulation was no different in the news coverage of events leading up to the War on Iraq. It seemed to the world that a war against Iraq would not be supported in the United States or abroad, by people or by governments. Doubts about the validity of WMD (Weapons of Mass Destruction) in Iraq and their potential risk to national security were strongly questioned. Concerns over the President's motives for such a proposed military advance against Saddam Hussein without United Nations' approval screamed like a siren over many a debate and analysis. Vast images of war protests and stories of human shields, laced with the Hollywood left's stiff disapproval of the Bush administration's war stance, filled the airwaves in a seemingly never-ending picture of a greater majority that had conceded that the idea of a war with Iraq as wrong, unjustified and downright nonsensical.

* "For me as an American, the most painful aspect of this is that I believe that [the Bush] administration has taken the events of September 11 and has manipulated

the grief of this country, and I think that's reprehensible."
—**Actor Dustin Hoffman** [4]

* "It's ludicrous to expect the whole world to follow what [George W. Bush and Tony Blair] want. ... America doesn't have the right to tell other people what to do. To say the whole world has to fall into line is you-know-what. I hope more people will rise up." —**Director Spike Lee.** [5]

* "[President Bush and his administration are] misguided ... and I think they are men who are possessed of evil. Mr. Bush is not a man of honor. I think he has a very selfish, arrogant point of view. I think he is interested in power. I think he believes his truth is the only truth."
—**Actor Harry Belafonte.** [6]

* "As an American, I've always been proud. I have a [U.S. flag] pin. I was embarrassed to wear it." —**Sen. Dianne Feinstein.** [7]

* "Yes, [President Bush] is racist. We all knew that, but the world is only finding it out now." —**Actor Danny Glover.** [8]

* "This nation will go into debt to destroy lives and people on the other side of the world while here at home we face

a financial disaster." —**Actor Ed Asner.**[9]

The position of many liberals regarding a potential war with Iraq seemed strictly political. Their anti-war contentions offered no logical alternatives for insuring the liberation and well-being of the Iraqi people. Their arguments suggested that there was no sense of urgency for the preservation of future human life in America, or abroad, because the potential threat of Saddam Hussein's regime was not that conclusively accurate. They argued that their position on "no war" demonstrated a higher concern for human life, even though Saddam's regime sanctioned torture, rape and murder as penalties for Iraqis who committed crimes, on top of hiding weapon arsenals and programs from United Nations weapons inspectors for 12 years, while also harboring and supporting terrorists and their activities.

It was typical how little coverage there was about people who weren't against a war with Iraq, who sided with the United States and Britain, and who believed that Saddam Hussein was hiding weapons of mass destruction. These types of reports were out there, but they did not receive the same coverage by the mainstream media. Such coverage would assist in making Bush appear logical, correct and justified in his conviction to wage a war on Iraq.

There were many reports that were far more Bush-supportive, news-accurate and factual than most of the

Reports of Mass Deception

anti-war rhetoric we were overwhelmed with in the mainstream news media's coverage leading up to the War on Iraq. Most countries were backing Bush on waging a war against Iraq with the exception of some of our supposed allies such as France, Germany and Russia.

The following is just a small list of headlines from the many news reports that failed to get an equal amount of coverage like the few hundred human shields who flew to Iraq story, which came across the airwaves giving the impression the majority felt as they did:

* "Saddam killed missile chief to thwart UN Team"[10]

* "Iraq: the threat of war–a letter to British Prime Minister, Tony Blair from 'Iraqi Exiles in U.K.'"[11]

* "Eight European leaders are as One with President Bush"[12]

* "East European Nations Back U.S. on Iraq"[13]

* "U.S. to have access to 21 countries in Iraq War: Armitage"[14]

* "Experts: Iraq has tons of chemical weapons"[15]

* "UN inspectors uncover proof of Saddam's nuclear

bomb plans"[16]

* "Saddam Killed Abu Nidal over al-Qaeda row"[17]

* "Iraq's Tie to al-Qaeda Terrorists, Airline Hijackings"[18]

* "The Sabah Khodada (former Iraqi captain) Interview in which he speaks of a terrorist training camp in Iraq"[19]

* "Iraq Nukes Sites Up and Atom Again"[20]

* "Exiles' 'liberate Iraq' plea"[21]

* "Iraq exiles back Blair's stance"[22]

It's uncanny how much the news media were questioning Bush's motives but not Saddam's. All the attention seemed to be on the Bush administration, while the questionable occurrences within Saddam's regime went seemingly unnoticed. How much attention was paid to General Muhammad Sa'id al-Darraj, Saddam's head missile engineer, who was assassinated 24 hours after talks with Saddam's officials about how to handle questions from United Nations weapons inspectors? [23]

"Personally, I was shocked while in the United States by how unquestioning the broadcast news media was during

Reports of Mass Deception

this war." —**BBC Director-General Greg Dyke.**[24]

Even after a brief anti-war and anti-Bush pause to show support for our troops at the very onset of major combat operations, it didn't take long for distorted coverage to rise to the top of the airwaves.

Tom Barrett, editor and publisher of *Conservative Truth*, an email-based newsletter and web site, *conservativetruth.org*, put it best in his March 24, 2003, column where he wrote about how news networks such as NBC, ABC, CBS, MSNBC, and CNN, were bombarding their viewers with distorted facts regarding the War on Iraq. He cited an example of this by his observation of images showing a few Iraqi civilian casualties being looped over and over again as an attempt to create the illusion that thousands have been killed.[25]

Despite the steady doses of anti-war and anti-Bush propaganda, the real majority of Americans would not be easily fooled any longer due to the horrific events on September 11, 2001. On that infamous day, the shroud of illusion was lifted. Amazingly, Americans seemed unified. Surprisingly, the majority of Americans found it appropriate and necessary to pray. Shockingly, most Americans worshipped and believed in God. Astoundingly, the majority of Americans were exposed for *not* holding the same liberal views as the mainstream media (or Hollywood, for that matter). On September 11th, and the weeks following it, the majority of

Americans spoke out, and all of us, including the entire world, saw us for what we really are: "One Nation, Under God, Indivisible with Liberty and Justice for all!"

Since then, the left-wing has tried feverishly to remind Americans that the majority still think, believe, and stand *for what they do*. Few were buying it, and the more they tried to sell it, the more ludicrous to everyone it seemed.

CHAPTER 2
Rally the Troops

Reports of Mass Deception

While the Bush administration continued prepping our nation and armed forces for the War on Iraq, the liberal extremists continued waging their anti-war and anti-Bush campaign in hopes that the support for the President and the war would diminish. At least that is how it came across prior, during, and after major combat operations. How can you take it as anything other than partisan rhetoric when the alternatives they debated over were as follows:

* Give Saddam more time to disarm, even though he's had 12 years to do so.
   (Saddam must think we're idiots. No wonder he didn't disarm.)

* Allow inspectors to keep searching for weapons that are moved to new locations daily.
   (Nothing like a good ol' diplomatic shell game.)

* Give peace a chance. If we demonstrate peace to Saddam, he may become a gentle soul.
   (This is the same tyrant who condoned the September 11, 2001 attacks on America.)

* Forget Iraq and focus on Iran and North Korea.
   (Whatever happened to following through with the issue at hand?)

Peter Chase

* Forget the whole thing and concentrate on the economy because that is the true terror. Most Americans resent the fact that we will be spending billions of dollars on a war instead of using this money for other, more important, domestic needs.
(There was no recognized scientific poll, at that time, which supported that. Why do you think that is?)

As the imminent War on Iraq converged, the mainstream media began to slowly clean up their tracks of promoting truth-twisting, anti-Bush propaganda for a brief period. They had to, because they knew the overwhelming public support for the President and our troops would not be able to remain hidden from our nation's eyes and ears, no matter what they tried to spin. The liberals understood this. The general public would not tolerate a non-paused campaign of liberal-spin designed solely to win votes for a Democratic presidential candidate in 2004 during a time when Americans needed to unite behind their troops in major combat operations.

In a poll for *FOX News Channel*, conducted by Opinion Dynamics Corporation just one week into the War on Iraq, 78% of Americans supported (66% "strongly") taking action to disarm Iraq and remove Saddam's regime while only18% opposed it. The results were not much different than from the results of a similar poll taken a month earlier which showed support for war at 71%.[1]

Reports of Mass Deception

The new spin was that we must support our troops. Many of the more media savvy liberals took this attitude when they read the current poll results from many conducted surveys which clearly showed overwhelming American support for the President and the War on Iraq shortly before major combat operations began. However, the liberals insinuated that Bush didn't have the majority of American support before the public realized that war was unavoidable. To back up that argument, they continually pointed to the reports showing anti-war and anti-Bush demonstrations in addition to other reports that raised doubt over Iraq's potential threat to national security and the lack of support for the U.S. around the world.

Was it true that there were many anti-war and anti-Bush protests? Yes, 100% true. However, it was also 100% true that there were many pro-war and pro-Bush rallies, but they got about 10 seconds of coverage on mainstream television and newspapers. On the contrary, we were bombarded with the coverage of the many college students across America who skipped classes to protest a war on Iraq. We saw clips of hundreds of kids, from various universities, marching up and down their campuses, waving signs with phrases similar to "No War" to "Bush is the Enemy." However, the liberal media failed to mention that a greater percentage of the student body, from every single one of those major universities that held protests, *did not* protest or skip classes. One of the major national student protests was dubbed "Books not Bombs," and was largely organized by the National Youth and Student Peace Coalition. They estimated between 30,000 to 50,000 students from high schools and colleges actively protested on campus. There are approximately 13.4 million high school and college students in the United States. If 50,000 students collectively protested, then how many didn't? At the University of Texas, 100 out of 49,000 students protested. At the University of California, 1,000 out of 37,000 protested. At the University of Colorado, 1,000 out of 26,000 protested. At the University of Wisconsin, 2,000 out of 41,000 protested. At Penn State University, 1,000 out of 41,000 protested.[2] If they reported those facts to you, the impact of the "Books not Bombs" anti-war rally would perhaps be looked upon by Americans as a dud. The real truth was that while a minority of students were against Bush's position on Iraq, more students were for it!

A vast array of vociferous insurgents echoed the assumption that the Iraqi people didn't want the United States messing in their affairs or with their regime–a theory that many war protesters and liberals argued.

"I am surprised to hear of all the anti-war demonstrations in the West. I wish that the demonstrators could spend just 24 hours in the place

Reports of Mass Deception

I have come from and see the reality of Iraq.
Fourteen lost years of my life. Nothing but bread
for food — darkness, filth, beatings, torture, killings,
bitterness and humiliation."—**Rafat Abdulmajeed
Muhammad, jailed for selling a roll of film to a
British journalist.**[3]

Perhaps the war protesters and their extreme liberal
cohorts meant to suggest Iraqis were in fear of Saddam's
regime and not fond of it? If they propagandized that
belief, that would have generated overwhelming
American sympathy for the Iraqi people immediately!

On Tuesday evening, March 18, 2003, just hours
before the much anticipated Presidential speech in which
Bush was expected to give Saddam one last chance to
avoid war, Democratic Senate Minority Leader Tom
Daschle aimed a controversial critique directly at
President Bush's efforts in diplomacy regarding Iraq. He
said before a group of union leaders that the Bush
administration had "forced"[4] the U.S. into war.

"I'm saddened - saddened that this President failed
so miserably at diplomacy that we're forced to go
to war," Daschle said. "I'm saddened that we have
to give up one life because this President couldn't
create the kind of diplomatic effort that was critical
for our country."[5]

Peter Chase

It is saddening - saddening that an elected official felt a need to express his strong objections publicly in what seemed to be only 48 hours before we sent thousands upon thousands of U.S. troops into a war with Iraq. On the other hand, perhaps he thinks it's saddening that people, such as myself, didn't understand his need to express discontent so closely to the brink of war? Liberals, like Daschle, oppose President Bush so passionately that they would sacrifice what I perceive is the higher moral and more upstanding position to take at a particular moment (not expressing malcontent), and replace it with an attempt to rally support against President Bush's decision and vent frustration.

Many other liberals spoke out and offered a different assessment of the current situation, thus realizing it was time to temporarily put aside the Bush-bashing before they entered into the realm of the point of no return with the majority of American people.

"It is time to come together and support our great American men and women in uniform and their Commander-in-Chief." —**Senator Joseph I. Lieberman.**[6]

According to *FOX News Channel*, a poll conducted by Opinion Dynamics Corporation showed 83% of Americans approved of attacking a building where Saddam was believed to be located (one of the first attacks in major combat operations) after Bush's 48-hour ultimatum to Saddam was not answered.[7]

When some liberals suggested that they supported the troops, but not their leader, did they realize that what they were saying made no sense? How can you really support the troops and their efforts, if you do not support their leader and the missions he commands them to carry out? Sounds like political gibberish designed to straddle both sides of the fence in an attempt to appease all Americans.

> "In a democracy, you have to express yourself and be honest with how you see the war unfold, and, as we've seen in other times in history, wars can be controversial," said Daschle. "We support strongly the troops, but there's a difference between the troops and the administration of a war."[8]

Case closed.

President Bush did not fail, by any means, in regard to trying to resolve the Iraq crisis in a diplomatic, peaceful fashion. It was the United Nations who failed diplomatically. The U.S. had bent-over-backwards giving Saddam Hussein every peaceful chance to disarm.

In the first Gulf War, we agreed to let Saddam stay in power under United Nations resolutions that imposed total and complete disarmament of WMD. After 12 years of diplomatic patty-cake and 16 meaningless United Nations resolutions, not only had Saddam not complied, but he continued to lie and deceive weapons inspectors.

In November 2002, President Bush decided to give Iraq, through the United Nations, even more undeserved time for a diplomatic solution by the proposed and unanimously passed United Nations Resolution 1441. Bush tried, but in the end, it was merely an exercise in political theater. Just like before the first Gulf War, and now 12 years later, Saddam Hussein never had intentions to willingly and peacefully disarm. Even in a last attempt at a peaceful solution, President Bush gave Saddam Hussein and his sons 48 hours to leave Iraq to avoid military conflict. No matter which way you look at it, President Bush exercised every possible solution to avoid war.

On the other hand, the United Nations unveiled itself for what it really is – a passive and ineffective body whose sole purpose is to emerge as the government which governs all governments. The United Nations cares only for its own agenda, which has everything in common with socialism and worldwide domination. This agenda consists of a system of global governance designed for people of every nation to rely on it for all their needs. The United Nations claims that this system is rooted in democracy. However, the "freedom" it offers is not the same as what we have in the United States. Our "freedom"

Reports of Mass Deception

was given to us by God in Whom we trust. It is a right that was fought for by our forefathers over 200 years ago. It is a right that gives us the privilege to manipulate government to suit our way of life, all of which is protected by our constitution. However, the United Nations' proposed system of global governance is designed to regulate nations and its people rather than the other way around. The United Nations' primary objectives are made very clear in the United Nations Charter for Global Democracy which was made public and signed by 56 nations on October 24, 1999.[9]

Despite last minute attempts of rallying around the Commander-in-Chief before war, the liberal extremists had already dug themselves into a hole which would take them many years to come out from. Since George W. Bush won the presidency over opponent Al Gore in the 2000 presidential election, the liberal extremists have made one foolish mistake after another, exposing objectives and goals that could be perceived as everything but that of helping Americans obtain an even better way of life. It seems that their primary focus is to generate anti-Bush rhetoric in an effort to gain Democratic Party support from the Oval Office on down. Because of this, if the economy crashes, it appears they win something because Bush looks bad. If the war on Iraq becomes a disaster, it appears they win because Bush looks bad. If we don't dismantle the al-Qaeda network, it appears they win because Bush looks bad. Do they actually desire this in their hearts? Hopefully not. However, their actions lead to the conclusion that perhaps, unknowingly, their "obsession" with discrediting Bush takes precedence over Americans benefiting directly from his administration's efforts.

CHAPTER 3
The War on Iraq

Reports of Mass Deception

Two weeks into the War on Iraq, the U.S. and coalition forces' overall strategic battle plan had encountered little to no *significant* resistance. It was going forward as scheduled, and it appeared, just as it did before the war started, that Saddam Hussein's regime was ultimately doomed. Iraqi forces had thus far shown no way of combating the U.S. and coalition assault effectively. Their military was scattered into small pockets which had been utterly overwhelmed as U.S. and coalition troops marched further into Iraq, securing more and more Iraqi territory on the way. The largest concentration of Republican Guard forces seemed to be lurking in the shadows of Baghdad. With their military bases and points of operation in that region being bombed heavily every night by carefully coordinated air strikes, their demise seemed to be inevitable as their weaponry, from guns to tanks, was all but obsolete. Many strategists and skeptics pondered what effective strategic maneuvers could Iraqi forces carry out successfully at this point? Many were suggesting that the ease that the U.S. and coalition forces were having was all a part of Saddam's master plan.

It has been debated that Saddam's war strategy from the onset was to create a political nightmare in the United States that would provoke the Bush administration to call for a cease-fire or, perhaps, cause Britain to back out. They had hoped to accomplish this by luring U.S. and coalition forces into urban warfare in Baghdad, thus prolonging the war, which would then rapidly increase the number of U.S. and coalition casualties. It was suggested that Saddam's regime also hoped to accomplish this by continually using their own people as human shields, thereby murdering them and then trying to disguise the atrocities as U.S. and coalition led warfare mistakes or planned attacks.

However, before they could even hope that their false war propaganda would actually start stirring more controversy among Americans and their allies with regard to whether this war would turn into another Vietnam, the last significant remnants of their regime were quickly disposed of.

To even *dream* that this war would become reminiscent of Vietnam is preposterous. But, many war skeptics draw this conclusion because of the remaining Baath Party extremists and terrorists left cowering inside the liberated Iraq five months after the end of major combat operations. These conclusions were made, while we were only approaching the half-year point of this postwar occupancy. We *are not* at the three-year mark and approaching year four! Also, there have been fewer than 500 American military deaths in total to this date since the war began and under 1,500 U.S. wounded. This is hardly comparable to the 58,202 U.S. deaths, the 304, 704 wounded in action, the 2,338 missing in action, and the 766 caught in action during the Vietnam War which

Reports of Mass Deception

lasted from 1961 until 1975 for the United States' part in whole.[1] Anyone who compares the War on Iraq to the Vietnam War is perhaps caught in a time warp. We're dealing with a small number of scattered terrorists in Baghdad, not the Vietcong!

Some analysts in the media suggested that perhaps Saddam's supposed urban warfare strategy was already working against us because the war had gone on for more than a week. History *clearly* dictates that any war, even if the opposition's military surrenders completely, takes longer than a week or two to complete.

On October 25, 1983, we invaded the 133 square-mile island of Grenada. That island took 10 days to conquer! When we invaded the small country of Panama on November 20, 1989, the operation lasted 15 days. In comparison, Iraq is 169,000 square miles and similar to the overall size of France. Considering the basic history of war and the factual demographics of Iraq, the initial assumption by some in the mainstream media that the war was going to be over in a few days baffles the mind.

The major combat operations in the Gulf War took 6 weeks, and that was heralded by many as a well executed strike. On the other hand, Kosovo, an arguably poorly executed campaign, took 8 weeks. Victory is going to take some time, poorly executed or not. Also, it took 44 days when the puissant German army invaded France on May 10, 1940, to defeat the French in World War II.

Peter Chase

Unless you are invading a small mass of land, it would seem impractical to envision winning a war in fewer than 2 weeks. It just doesn't happen.

During the major combat operations, many of the Iraqi oil wells in southern Iraq had been secured, and a large portion of the country had already been overtaken and was under the control of U.S. and coalition forces within the first two weeks. The nightly air strikes on Baghdad and other significant cities had clearly minimized and compromised the level of force that the Republican Guard could attempt to mount against our troops as we drew closer to the targets then at hand. No matter what some reported in the mainstream media to the contrary, Iraqi resistance was futile. Saddam's reign of terror was nearing its end, the government in Iraq had lost almost all control, and the Iraqi people were only mere weeks away from liberation.

The days following the momentous removal of the 40-foot statue of Saddam in Firdos Square in the heart of Baghdad on April 9, 2003, had been the worst kind of agony for extreme left-wing liberals since George W. Bush was officially declared President over Al Gore. Soon after that very tight election, they were suddenly faced with the utter truth that their post-election propaganda (supposed claims of disenfranchised voters due to a number of ludicrous reasons such as rocket-science type ballot directions and hanging chads) failed

Reports of Mass Deception

to illegally elect Al Gore. Now, a little over two years later, they are once again faced with the undeniable truth that their grand sheaf of anti-Bush/anti-war rhetoric had been revealed for what it was—partisan-based, illogical analysis given for the sole purpose of taking away support for the Bush administration.

First of all, one of the many laughable points of debate was whether or not the Iraqi people really wanted to be freed. It's human nature to want to be free. We are born with it! We do not need to be born in freedom or experience life in America to understand what freedom is. We are all born with the desire and will to be free. Even animals are born with the will to be free. The liberals soon realized that this argument was entirely too flimsy, so they spun it a couple of other ways.

Various mainstream media reporters began asking Iraqi people, before the fall of the regime, if they wanted to be freed from Saddam's rule. To paraphrase the answers that were reported, they said, "No!" Of course they said, "No!" They lived in Iraq, under a brutal dictatorship at the time. One wrong word, especially against Saddam, and they could have kissed their life good-bye, or worse yet, their spouse's or children's.

Liberals also advocated that the Iraqi people wanted to be freed, but they wanted to free themselves without interference from the United States. Sounds politically viable that perhaps some Iraqis could feel this way, doesn't it? However, every place that U.S. and coalition forces have liberated from Saddam's regime have thus far resulted in citizens dancing, shouting, and rejoicing. The liberated people of Baghdad were no different.

There were hundreds of quotes taken by reporters in Baghdad from the Iraqi people once the 40-foot statue of Saddam was brought down in central Baghdad on April 9, 2003.

"We are relieved because for years we lived in anxiety and fear." **—Shamoun George, a resident of Baghdad's Karrada district, as American troops entered the area.**[2]

"I'm 49, but I never lived a single day." **—Yusuf Abed Kazim, a Baghdad man who pounded the statue's pedestal with a sledgehammer.**[3]

"Now my son can have a chance in life." **—Bushra Abed, pointing to her 2-year-old son, Ibrahim.**[4]

There were many news reports that attempted to tell the story of the incredible feeling, mood, and jubilant atmosphere of this historic moment. The following are some headlines and subheadings of articles reporting on the event:

Reports of Mass Deception

* "Marines Help Topple Statue; Baghdadis Loot City" [5]

* "Iraqis Celebrate As U.S. Takes Baghdad"[6]

* "U.S. Hails End of Saddam Era: Statue Toppled in Central Baghdad; Crowds Cheer U.S. Marines; Forces Focus on Tikrit"[7]

However, there is always an "expert" way to spin this in a negative light. The very next day, some mainstream news media analysts looked at the subsequent looting in Iraq as a powerful indication that the Iraqi people don't know what freedom is or what to do with it. They used "looting in Baghdad" as a means to justify their point that Iraqis don't understand or want freedom. Ridiculous! There are many instances of looting due to riots in America every year! Rush Limbaugh described the looting in Baghdad as "surgical looting."[8] The Iraqis were initially only looting the places where Saddam's regime had significant precedence. Also, they were doing it in joy and happiness, not in anger. They weren't smashing people over the heads with various objects like they do in many American riots. For three decades, Saddam stole the wealth of the Iraqi people, and one can conclude that this looting was only part of their celebration, which was long overdue.

Peter Chase

"Opponents of the war with Iraq who, with thinly veiled bigotry, said that Muslims just don't want freedom, are looking at the scenes of 'surgical looting' in Baghdad as proof they were right."—**Rush Limbaugh.**[9]

On April 14, 2003, just days after the liberation of millions of Iraqis, House Minority Leader Nancy Pelosi said, "I think that it's very important to have as pillars of our foreign policy promoting democratic values [and] stopping the proliferation of weapons of mass destruction. But I think that there are other ways to go about it than to have thousands of people killed on both sides."[10]

To this day, there are still under 500 U.S. fatalities from the War on Iraq and the postwar. However, over 3,000 Americans died on September 11, 2001. The terrorists declared war on us, and there is no other way to go about defeating them other than taking them out along with the countries who harbor and support them.

The 2000 Presidential election in which George W. Bush edged Al Gore out of the presidency revealed the eccentric socialist-based objectives of extreme liberal activists. They never have gotten over that defeat, and they have been on an ongoing childish rampage against Bush and his administration ever since. The debate and percentages against Bush and this war weren't anything more than they were in previous wars with other commanders-in-chief. The amount of protesting was consistent, along with the amount of support. However, this time around, it was clear that the viciousness of the protesting against the war and our President has gone to a entirely new level.

The cat was let out of the bag when liberal extremists missed out on having Al Gore as President. It was so close; that defeat hurt so badly. Because of this, and a lack of common sense and fortitude to deal with it, they have, perhaps unknowingly, exposed their true colors for what they are.

It is too late for them to get behind the President now. They had their chance, and they blew it. That is why the American public began hearing fewer and fewer important and non-fragmented news reports about the situations associated with the war. They despise Bush so much, that it seems they would rather see him fail, than have him succeed at something that benefits not only 25 million Iraqis, but Americans at home.

CHAPTER 4
The Bleak Postwar

Reports of Mass Deception

According to a Yahoo.com article on April 17, 2003, by Associated Press writer Jim Abrams, Democratic House Majority Leader Nancy Pelosi "cultivated harmony"[1] among Democrats in the House of Representatives by assuring them that minorities and women would start being promoted to key committees, and that rural work groups would be established to provide a voice for more conservative members within the Democratic Party.

Wow! If only Nancy and her supporters were running the Senate—Miguel Estrada would certainly have gotten the nod to serve as a judge on the U.S. Circuit Court of Appeals. The then-current filibuster against this Hispanic minority would have by no means been tolerated! Instead, her liberal allies on the Senate made sure that Mr. Estrada would not advance.

On and on, this type of double standard continues to spin through our culture, revealing the folly of the far left's campaign that is supposedly for the people, and only for the people.

Folly? Absolutely!

"I have absolutely no regret about my vote on this war," Nancy Pelosi told reporters at a weekly briefing.[2] She went on to question the cost in human lives, the cost to our nation's budget and the cost to the War on Terrorism.

Peter Chase

Americans need to remember that our enemies spared no expense planning the 9/11 attacks, and neither should we to protect the innocent people of this great nation. Can we really put a price tag on the cost of freedom? If preventing further 9/11-type attacks means spending 100, 200 or 500 billion dollars, then so be it. Consider this scenario: you have a small gas leak in your house. You get an estimate to repair the leak that is in the thousands of dollars range. After looking at your bank accounts and budget, you realize that fixing this leak will be a struggle for you financially. You can either tolerate it and hope the small gas leak doesn't amount to anything more hazardous while you search for ways to deal with the problem more cost effectively, or you can fix the problem right away before the damages amount to hundreds of thousands of dollars as would be the case if the house blew up. Despite the fact that the initial price to repair the leak is costly and creates financial setbacks, to do otherwise would be potentially far more disastrous. There is an old saying—"You get what you pay for!" Thank God, President Bush is our leader during such times as these.

Where are the terrorist attacks on our nation? Who now walks in fear, Americans or terrorists? Who is in control of our nation's freedom? The American people are, thanks to the Bush administration's relentless, unwavering effort to vanquish these foul foes. Bush

Reports of Mass Deception

actually did what he said he would do! His promise to the American people to fight terrorism and protect our freedom, at any cost, was not shallow. He didn't change his tune when the heat was poured on. He didn't base his decision to invade Afghanistan and Iraq on whether or not it would help his re-election campaign in 2004. He based his decisions on what he promised the American people, and what he vowed to do as President of the United States.

Have you noticed that we have our country back? Since the War on Iraq began, I personally have never felt safer in America since before September 11, 2001. There's no bargaining with killer bees. There is no compromise with serial killers. There is no drawn-line that would be honored by relentless sharks. And there is no treaty, as proven after 12 years and 16 resolutions, that would be honored by a madman hell-bent on the annihilation of the U.S., and the obliteration of all freedom. Syria, Cuba, North Korea, and a host of other dictatorships now understand, with certainty, that harboring and supporting terrorists, and/or threatening the freedom of the American people, will not be tolerated.

Countries who support terror can no longer hide behind the United Nations, which in my eyes, is the greatest harborer of such activity. Like the Democrats' filibustering against Miguel Estrada, the United Nations only holds true to their supposed convictions as long as it doesn't benefit a person, group or party that holds an opposing political view to theirs. They only mean what they say, if it doesn't interfere with their political aspirations down the line. Resolution 1441 was certainly far from vague on all points regarding the consequences of failed disarmament by Saddam Hussein. The resolution was unanimously passed, but some, as we now all know, didn't really agree with the resolutions, despite signing off on it. It was just the thing to do politically at the moment. Are these deceitful nations really our allies?

We don't need allies such as France, Germany and Russia to grant us permission to protect our interests. The Bush administration made that very clear when we invaded Iraq without United Nations approval. Dictators like Fidel Castro of Cuba, Bashar Assad of Syria, and Kim Jong Il of North Korea are frightened by the prospect that the U.S. can no longer be collared and chained by the bureaucracy of the United Nations. No longer can they hide behind the United Nations whose constitution has little in common with American democracy. The United Nations' ultimate objective is to establish a one-world socialistic government, a goal many conservatives believe to be rooted in a Soviet-Communist influenced constitution. Evolving from the League of Nations, the United Nations was first formed, in part, by Alger Hiss, a former State Department official who worked under President Roosevelt's administration. Hiss was appointed

Reports of Mass Deception

the United Nations' first Secretary General in 1945 and was later accused of being a Soviet spy by evidence derived from the famous "Pumpkin Papers."[3] The "Pumpkin Papers" were uncovered by Whittaker Chambers, an ex-Soviet spy who led investigators to a hollow pumpkin which contained 5 rolls of 35 mm film. This film, along with 65 pages of retyped secret State Department documents, four pages in Hiss's own handwriting, would later turn out to be the decisive evidence which convinced jurors to render a guilty verdict against Hiss of perjury for denying he was a Soviet spy on January 20, 1950. Liberals, in general, typified this verdict as a social inequity, characterizing the evidence against Hiss as a dubious conservative conspiracy contrived to generate distrust and skepticism relating to the Democratic Party among Americans. Many conservatives feel that the "Pumpkin Papers" along with the "VENONA files" (decoded cables sent from Soviet agents in the United States to Moscow) transcript from a March 30, 1945 transmitted message, provide concrete evidence that Hiss was indeed a Soviet spy, a claim Hiss contested until his death on November 15, 1996.

As the months of postwar Iraq mounted, the Bush-bashing also mounted to epic proportions. Obviously, the unwarranted barrage of Bush-bashing was an attempt to have him lose as much public support as possible as we inch closer to the 2004 election. It is almost inconceivable that he will lose. It appears that the left is aware of that possibility and is trying to turn the tide against him by the clever use of defamation propaganda spotlighted by the liberal-controlled mainstream news media. However, liberals would be better served by approaching this matter laced-up in more "sensible shoes." The way to beat Bush is not by criticizing the war and attempting to hide all the positive facts; it is by presenting the people with an honest and genuine alternative to what this administration has offered. If it's done in good taste and makes sense, people will respect it and pay more attention to it and quite possibly, vote for it.

The Bush-bashing combined with the mainstream media's relentless coverage of a tainted truth regarding the many aspects in the progress on the War on Terrorism, and, more specifically, the postwar in Iraq is the most captivating entertainment on the airwaves. The candidates in the Democratic Presidential Primary continue to actuate this deception of supposed Iraq calamity and utter failure in their many less-than-enchanting, support-seeking speeches. The familiar theme is an overwhelming mocking of President Bush and his supposed military debacle leading the War on Iraq. They are riding this soon-to-crash wave of Bush-bashing instead of focusing on their usual extreme-liberal agenda which includes support for policies such as the theory that every problem can be

Reports of Mass Deception

solved by taxing and the creation of bigger government. In turn, this creates, in many underclass circles, what Ann Coulter described so eloquently in her September 3, 2003, column, "a permanent underclass of aspiring criminals knifing one another between having illegitimate children and collecting welfare checks."[4]

The Bush-bashing is distasteful. Consider the following statements, which are just a couple taken from an enormous hodgepodge of the most petty political bantering one can ever hear amongst dignified men seeking your vote for the office of President of the United States of America:

* (regarding Bush's economic policies) "who do voodoo economics" —**Rev. Al Sharpton.**[5] (a reference to Bush Sr.'s 1980 denunciation of President Reagan's economic plans as "voodoo economics.")

* "In two short years, George W. Bush has taught us what the 'W' stands for — wrong. Wrong for our children, wrong for our parents, wrong for our values. Wrong, wrong, wrong for America." —**Sen. John Edwards**[6]

Juvenile digs and the propagandizing of tainted truths are not going to win any one of them a four-year stint in the White House. Americans want to hear more civilized, thought-provoking debates on issues from would-be commanders-in-chief, not professional wrestling style trash-talk!

These reduntant shots at Bush have landed so far outside the foul pole, that liberal icons, such as Senator Hillary Clinton (D-NY), seem to have recently been forced to step up to the plate and subtly de-bash Bush on some of the War on Iraq debates in an attempt to level the liberal-swing and get some non-fantastical issues on base. Senator Clinton said that the CIA intelligence regarding Saddam's WMD and nuclear capability have been consistent during the last three administrations, thus making the War on Iraq not so unjustifiable.[7] And she also mentioned that if WMD are not discovered, that the CIA intelligence needs to be scrutinized, not necessarily the President who is merely acting on what is presented before him.[8]

September 2003's United Nations speech delivered by President Bush in New York City is a perfect example of media truth-twisting. Many of the reports summarizing his speech suggested that our President was almost begging for United Nations support and forgiveness, standing at the podium before the group of anti-American socialists like a naughty child facing his elders after committing crimes of defiance. If anything, Bush was living up to his pre-war promise that he would allow the United Nations to assist in the rebuilding of Iraq once major combat operations were completed. He didn't just

Reports of Mass Deception

impetuously decide to crawl on his hands and knees to the United Nations. He had every intention of including them in the rebuilding of Iraq, because he felt, from the beginning, that their assistance in the rehabilitation would be of great value and importance. Was there *any time* he said that the United Nations would *not* be asked to participate whatsoever in Iraq's rebuilding process?

Here are a few of the headlines, subheadings, and excerpts used in the coverage of the United Nations speech:

* Bush UN speech persuades few: World leaders, Democrats deride President's address as too little, too late"[9]

* Under fire at UN, Bush rejects early Iraq transfer"[10]

* U.S. slammed for bypassing UN over Iraq"[11]

The liberal-controlled mainstream news media's aired and published coverage of this address to the United Nations General Assembly would lead one to believe that Bush was asking for forgiveness for going to war with Iraq, rather than addressing the United Nations. It's amazing how people spin this. Bush basically told the United Nations, in graceful, civilized cowboy fashion, exactly what he expects from them, nothing more, and nothing less.

Peter Chase

"America is working with friends and allies on a new Security Council resolution, which will expand the UN role in Iraq. As in the aftermath of other conflicts, the United Nations should assist in developing a constitution, in training civil servants, and conducting free and fair elections," stated Bush during his speech to the UN.[12]

Read the entire transcript from his speech yourself at the official White House web site, www.whitehouse.gov, archived under news releases. Don't believe the spin!

The United Nations does not bear America's core interests at heart. President Bush clearly exposed that fact when he was forced to form a coalition of allies for the War on Iraq without United Nations approval. Besides that, perhaps President Bush has other reasons for limiting the United Nations' role in postwar Iraq. Case in point: the United Nations and their affiliates, the European Union (E.U.) and the Organization for Security and Cooperation in Europe (OSCE), were put in charge of the rebuilding process in Kosovo after the U.S. and NATO (North Atlantic Treaty Organization) bombed the Serbian region a little over four and a half years ago. Even though the bombings didn't touch the province's power plants, Kosovo's electricity to this day is cut every four hours, for two hour periods, 24 hours a day, 7 days a week.[13]

Reports of Mass Deception

Ironically, this ethnic Albanian province once repressed by genocidal maniac Slobodan Milosevic, was also once a proud exporter of power to neighboring countries before the NATO bombings chapter of the Kosovo War. What's more ironic is that power needs to be imported to them, but they have little funds to do so because the Kosovors are living in economic disaster despite the upwards of $9 billion disbursed towards its reconstruction effort–funds already spent in totality by the United Nations, E.U., and the OSCE. On top of this, the United Nations still has not convicted Slobodan Milosevic for war crimes and atrocities against humanity. I do hope if we capture bin Laden and Hussein, that it won't take half a decade to find these terrorists guilty. The victims of all these madmen didn't get the privilege of years in bureaucracy to pacify them before their sentences were inevitably carried out! Furthermore, some argue that Kosovo is not that much better from where it was over four years ago. The roadway system is ragged, the overall infrastructure is a dysfunctional mess, and it is uncertain whether Kosovo will emerge as a democratic state.

On the other hand, in Iraq the U.S. has already reopened 22 universities, 43 colleges and technical schools, and almost all primary and secondary schools in just a few months after major combat operations. 1500 of those schools have been refurbished. The U.S. has also established an Independent Central Bank, a police department, and a new government–all of which are functioning. After World War II, the U.S. occupancy in Germany and Japan performed similar tasks as they transformed the regions from despotisms to democracies, both of which eventually went on to experience thriving economies. Weighing in these simple, yet factual comparisons, logic concludes that the United Nations' limited role in Iraq is a good thing.

As far as the effort in Iraq being botched and failed, it is quite the contrary, especially to the people of Iraq. In the beginning of September 2003, the Gallup Organization conducted 70-minute private interviews with more than 1,000 Iraqis in what they called "the first rigorous and scientifically conducted sampling of public sentiment in Iraq."[14] The scientific survey revealed that 62% of Iraqis in Baghdad felt their liberation was worth any pain and suffering they endured due to the War on Iraq.[15] The poll results also showed that 67% believed their country would be improved in five years. 36% had favorable views regarding the U.S. led Coalition Provisional Authority, while 43% gave it only fair views and only 19% perceived it as bad.[16] It is not surprising that the Iraqis support our military's postwar efforts in their country, especially since they need us there to help wipe out the remaining Baath Party resistance and other such terrorist groups. Did liberal extremists think that pockets of murderous fanatics would not arise against

Reports of Mass Deception

coalition forces after the major combat operations subsided? Did they really think we would enter a country the size of Iraq with its enormous population and have an instant "candyland" democratic state a week, a month, or a year later?

U.S. Rep. Jim Marshall (D-Ga.) of Macon, a Vietnam combat veteran and a member of the House Armed Services Committee, visited Iraq during the summer of 2003 to see for himself what was actually going on during the aftermath of major combat operations. He noted that the Pentagon's reports of the progress we are making in Iraq are far more accurate than the mainstream news media's interpretation of it.[17]

He also observed that "falsely bleak Iraq news" is a serious problem for the U.S. occupancy as it discourages Iraqi cooperation which he felt was the "key" to success, or failure, in Iraq.[18]

In response to questions submitted online as part of "Ask the White House," a live, public forum found on the White House web site, Dan Senor, a senior adviser to the U.S. Presidential Envoy in Iraq, shared his assessment of the situation in Iraq from his own observations in the country during the first six months of the War on Iraq with guests on its web site forum on October 9, 2003.

"Hospitals are open. Schools are open. Children are back at school. Iraqis are taking more and more responsibility for their security. There is a flourishing free press with over 160 Iraqi newspapers that have started up since liberation," Mr. Senor said. "Ninety-five percent of the country is at peace and returning to normal daily life."[19] Senor also said, "The overwhelming majority of Iraqi people have embraced the liberation and are grateful for all we are doing to reconstruct their country."[20]

On October 27, 2003, the mainstream news media jumped all over the car bombing incidents which struck the Red Cross headquarters and 3 police stations in Iraq. Using biased, colorful metaphors, it made the tragedy appear more like an epic catastrophe mirroring Pearl Harbor. Words such as "bloodiest," "devastated," "thunderous," and "bloodbath" glistened throughout an Associated Press article which appeared on AOL entitled, "Ramadan Begins With Bloodbath in Baghdad."[21] The journalistic article, which was supposed to be unbiased since it was a report and not a commentary, feature, or opinion column, reported that it appeared, to the writer, that the attacks were perhaps Saddam loyalists or Islamic extremists. Though that's surely believable, the article went on to mention that some believe this resistance also included Iraqis who simply resent the U.S. military in their country, or they are upset with what they see as

Reports of Mass Deception

U.S. brutality against their friends. There is no mention of who believes this, but somehow this made it into this report. Perhaps the article should have also included that some believe aliens from outer space have spiritually demonized the U.S. military still occupying there.

This is why *FOX News Channel* gets such high ratings. The main page headline on their web site linking to the article read, "Baghdad Blasts Kill at Least 35."[22] Notice how *FOX News Channel* used the word, "blast" rather than "bloodshed," a far more accurate description. The *Los Angeles Times* ran with a headline that read, "Baghdad Rocked by Bombs; Dozens Dead."[23] Did Elvis have a concert? Perhaps they should have led with a headline such as "Baghdad gets Shook, Rattled and Rolled by Bombs."

On the same day, under AOL News in a section entitled "The Daily Pulse," there was a poll question which basically asked what people thought of Defense Secretary Donald Rumsfeld's style and if he would help or hinder Bush in his 2004 bid for a second term. Next to this poll was a little blurb which insinuated that Rumsfeld fell from a "star" amongst Americans to a "failure" because things have not gone "smoothly" in Iraq and now he is "paying the price."[24] This is another classic example of crafty liberal deception. It subtly paints a picture to the non-informed reader that Rumsfeld failed, and the War on Iraq is now similar to the Vietnam War, and all is hopeless.

The liberally-controlled mainstream news media appears hell-bent on trying desperately to convince the American people that Bush, Rumsfeld and the rest of the administration failed miserably in Iraq. They will birth every possible truth-twisting angle from desired parts of factual news, to spin their web of mass deception designed to capture the fool and the fool who follows him.

As long as we are rebuilding Iraq, the skeptics will insist the War on Iraq hasn't ended and is reminiscent of a Vietnam War quagmire. This is because every single terrorist attack in Iraq will be reported as part of the War on Iraq when it really should be dubbed as an act in the War on Terrorism. In ten years, if there is a terrorist attack in Iraq, rest assured it will be said to be part of the War on Iraq. After President Bush declared the major combat operations over back in May 2003, Saddam was defeated, his government overthrown, and a new democratic government was established during this current postwar—all incomparable to the results of the Vietnam War which we didn't win. All these reports regarding U.S. soldiers killed in isolated incidents around Baghdad are a clear indication that terrorists are in Iraq. These attacks are not coming from the Iraqi civilians, standing up against the U.S. occupation who are insuring them of a democratic, free future. They are coming from a small number of terrorists, which include remaining Baath Party loyalists

Reports of Mass Deception

who are terrorists, just as their former leader Saddam was.

According to an article in the November 10, 2003 issue of the *Weekly Standard* entitled, "Distinguishing Foe from Foe," by Stephen F. Hayes, General Ray Odierno, commander of the 4th Armored Division in Iraq, said that religious extremists pose the greatest threat to the U.S. led coalition occupancy in Iraq, and 95% of that resistance–which is estimated by the Pentagon to be around 3,000 and by military officials in Iraq as being even smaller at only several hundred–is composed of former Baath Party loyalists.[25] Once these terrorists are flushed out, the reports of isolated attacks will decrease drastically. This is not a large number of estimated resistant forces, and it is laughable to hear the postwar occupancy in Iraq being related to the Vietnam War. There, we were guerilla-style fighting hundreds of thousands of North Vietnamese and Vietcong soldiers combined. Of these soldiers, 444,000 were killed in action which subsequently resulted in the aforementioned 58,202 U.S. deaths, and 304,704 U.S. wounded in action. As of this writing, fewer than 500 U.S. soldiers have died since the onset of the War on Iraq, 115 of which died during major combat operations. Are the postwar fatalities a result of guerrilla warfare? Not exactly, but terrorism is very similar to the sneaky, cowardly way guerilla warfare is orchestrated. Actually, it is far more cowardly. That is what modern warfare is all about because that is how terrorists fight! However, that does not make the postwar occupancy in Iraq like Vietnam. Perhaps, if Northern Iraq was controlled and under the authority of Baath Party loyalists numbering in the tens of thousands, then we could start looking at Vietnam comparisons. Unless such an unlikely event happens, they do not have dominion anywhere in Iraq, and their pathetic little band of rogue terrorists is shrinking more and more each day thanks to the diligence, service and sacrifice of our troops.

On Sunday, November 2, 2003, the Associated Press reported that a U.S. Chinook helicopter was shot down in central Iraq, killing 16 GI's and wounding 20.[26] This is a tragic event, as it is when any U.S. soldier dies, be it in Iraq, Afghanistan, or anywhere. However, that incident was not the Battle of Gettysburg, as most of these reports would lead you to believe. We are not fighting an army, the Republican Guard or the Vietcong. Simply put, in the Middle East, there will be terrorist attacks until all terrorist groups are flushed out and vanquished. If we had invaded Syria or Iran instead of Iraq, we would then be facing the similar postwar challenges we face now.

Military officials near the Syrian border claim that jihadists are getting into the country of Iraq.[27] They are not coming for a friendly vacation, and until the War on Terrorism progresses to the point of a worldwide victory over Terrorism, there will be car bombings and other attacks taking place in the Middle East in areas like Iraq,

Reports of Mass Deception

Israel, or any place that supports freedom in that region. Just like in Afghanistan, no matter where you put U.S. soldiers in the Middle East, they are going to get attacked during this War on Terrorism. The last thing they want is for their Great Satan (the U.S.) to foil their future plans of destroying freedom throughout the world.

There are many reports of mass deception designed to discredit the Bush administration for the sole purpose of turning the American people against him in the hope that Americans would vote him out in favor of a new President that would have supposedly handled the War on Terrorism, while also balancing our many domestic issues, better than Bush has thus far. Whatever the liberal extremists spin, they cannot shroud the simple fact that the economy, be it unstable as it has been since it was handed down to Bush in January 2001, is showing signs of recovery in the midst of this War on Terrorism. Couple that with the fact that *no* terrorist attacks have taken place on our soil since September 11, 2001, who really could have done a better job than Bush has done considering the hand he was dealt since that tragic day? Our country is safer, our people are more free, our economy is steadily showing indications of healing amidst a war, and the terrorists are frantically running for their lives—instead of us having to run for ours!

CHAPTER 5
I Want My WMD

Reports of Mass Deception

Where are these so-called Weapons of Mass Destruction (WMD)?

That's the resounding question coming forth from skeptics' mouths these days. "They want proof, not leads," much like what Admiral Ozzel demanded of Captain Piett in the Imperial Death Squadron prior to the Battle of Hoth in "Star Wars V: The Empire Strikes Back." And, much like science fiction, many war skeptic extremists continue to try to convince themselves, and the public, that President Bush is the real problem, and Saddam was unjustly attacked and not given sufficient time to work with his many supporters at the United Nations.

Supporters? Yes! After 12 years and 16 resolutions, you would think that the United Nations would spend less time criticizing the Bush administration's position on Iraq and more time finding fault with Saddam's regime. Perhaps Saddam was always less of a threat to the United Nations than the "land of the free and the home of the brave," the greater obstacle in their socialist agenda to achieve a one-world government, with a one-world tax, a one-world court, and a one-world medical plan, with a world population solely dependent on this one-world government for all their needs—from poverty-prevention—to the raising of their children. The United Nations' way of making the world a better place is to convince everyone that the general populace, of any country, doesn't know what is best for themselves, their children or their lives. The last thing that the United Nations wants is a United States-type of democracy established in Iraq. However, they wouldn't mind implementing their own democracy where the Iraqis could be led along their entire lives like lemmings.

Here are some of the ambitions of the United Nations for the 21st century made clear in their United Nations Charter for Global Democracy which was made public and signed by 56 nations on October 24, 1999:[1]

* Consolidation of all international agencies under the sole authority of the United Nations.

* United Nations regulation of all transnational corporations and financial institutions.

* Independent revenue sources for the Unitd Nations such as a "Tobin Tax."

* The elimination of veto power by the Security Council.

* A United Nations army.

* United Nations registration of all military arms.

* Worldwide compliance with all United Nations human rights treaties.

Reports of Mass Deception

* Creation of the International Criminal Court as a remedy of social injustice to individuals.

* Creation of an International Environmental Court.

* The elimination of all debt owed by poor countries.

Much like the United Nations, many liberals in this country are firing at the Bush administration claiming we did not have sufficient evidence of Saddam's WMD to warrant the War on Iraq. The many reports of mass deception regarding weapons of mass destruction are an attempt to mislead the American people into believing that the War on Iraq was simply an act of warmongering and bullying at an enormous and unnecessary expense just for the cowboy kicks of George W. Bush.

Before we continue, let's get one thing straight— the War on Iraq is part of the War on Terrorism. When those planes crashed into the World Trade Center towers, the Pentagon and in an open field in Pennsylvania on September 11, 2001, that was the day that *war* was declared against the United States. It became clear how vulnerable we are and how much more seriously we needed to guard our own borders. Can you imagine if those terrorists also had chemical weapons on those planes as well? How much more difficult do you think it would be for a terrorist cell to compromise our water, food, and air supply with chemical agents, than hijacking 4 planes at one time? Can you imagine the Iraqi regime, who had used biological weapons before, selling them to terrorists? No one likes to imagine these things, but in the interest of national security, our government must consider these possibilities after the seemingly impossible attacks of September 11, along with the abundant evidence of Saddam's WMD programs provided by various intelligence agencies, which include not only our own CIA, but the United Nations' intelligence agency (UNSCOM), and Russian, German, and British intelligence agencies just to name a few. The haters of America, which include Saddam, declared war on this great nation on 9/11, and President Bush wasn't about to dilly-dally around with the United Nations to obtain permission to take out any country which harbors, supports and deals in terrorism.

"Under this view, even in the face of a specific stated agreed upon danger, the mere objection of even one foreign government would be sufficient to prevent us from acting," said Vice President Dick Cheney to the Heritage Foundation in regards to UN approval to go to war with Iraq. He added, "This view reflects a deep confusion about the requirements of our national security. Though often couched in high sounding terms of unity and

Reports of Mass Deception

cooperation, it is a prescription for perpetual disunity and obstructionism."[2]

In a speech during his visit to Portsmouth, N.H., on October 9, 2003, President Bush further explained his reasoning for going to war with Iraq without United Nations approval.

> "I acted because I was not about to leave the security of the American people in the hands of a madman," he explained. "I was not about to stand by and wait and trust in the sanity and restraint of Saddam Hussein.
> "So in one of the swiftest and most humane military campaigns in history, we removed the threat," he added.[3]

If we never find stockpiles of WMD in Iraq, the mere discovery of intent and the proof of purposeful deception to United Nations weapons inspectors, accented by the fact that Saddam used biological weapons before on his own people, is justification enough for the War on Iraq.

> "When I left office, there was a substantial amount of biological and chemical material unaccounted for. That is, at the end of the first Gulf War, we knew

what he had. We knew what was destroyed in all the inspection processes and that was a lot. And then we bombed with the British for four days in 1998. We might have gotten it all; we might have gotten half of it; we might have gotten none of it. But we didn't know. So I thought it was prudent for the President to go to the UN and for the UN to say you got to let these inspectors in, and this time if you don't cooperate the penalty could be regime change, not just continued sanctions."—**former U.S. President Bill Clinton, July 22, 2003** [4]

The following is a basic list of the claims of Iraq's chemical and biological weapons capabilities from a September 2002 dossier produced by the British government and submitted to Parliament:[5]

* The continued production of chemical and biological agents.

* Military plans for use of the chemical and biological weapons.

* Command and control operations in place to use chemical and biological weapons.

Reports of Mass Deception

* Deployed mobile production of biological warfare agents.

* Designed illegal programs for securing and hiding materials for WMD.

A study by the International Institute for Strategic Studies and a CIA dossier produced shortly afterwards were largely consistent with Britain's assessment of Saddam's chemical weapon capabilities.[6]

The following are headlines and brief excerpts from two UNSCOM investigative reports, that can be found on the *Washington Post's* web site, which reveal some of the useful, compiled intelligence regarding Iraq's WMD before the War on Iraq:

1. "UNSCOM Tracks Terror Weapons: United Nations arms inspectors and the International Atomic Energy Agency say Iraq continues to play a deadly shell game that conceals many of the most dangerous weapons that survived the 1991 Gulf War."[7]

2. "The Unconventional Arsenal: The United Nations and United States suspect Iraq still holds dangerous amounts of chemical and biological weapons of mass destruction. The types and amounts listed here are what Iraq says it possessed over the last seven years. Iraq insists the

chemical and biological stockpiles have been destroyed; the United Nations disputes that."[8]

Before Bush unveiled his serious plans to deal with Saddam by the use of force, the overall liberal view on the 12 years of compiled intelligence regarding Iraq's WMD current program, future programs and stockpiles, was that there was more than ample evidence to conclude that Iraq was a very real threat to homeland security.

"The Iraqi regime and its weapons of mass destruction represent a clear threat to world security. This danger has been explicitly recognized by the UN"—**Letter by eight European leaders in support of the United States.**[9]

"Of course they [Saddam's regime] have no credibility. If they had any, they certainly lost it in 1991. I don't see that they have acquired any credibility."—**former Chief United Nations Weapons Inspector Hans Blix.**[10]

"Some way, someday, I guarantee you he'll [Saddam] use the arsenal [WMD]."—**President Bill Clinton in 1998.**[11]

David Kay, the CIA operative in charge of the investigation of finding Iraq's WMD said the following

Reports of Mass Deception

in his Senate briefing on October 2, 2003: "At this time there is substantial evidence of an intent of senior level Iraqi officials, including Saddam, to continue production at some future point of time, of weapons of mass destruction."[12]

Is this not enough for the war skeptics? Instead of praising the Bush administration for obviously making the *right* decision to take out Saddam, the reports most Americans heard from the media screeched with a recurring theme which read similarly to, "No WMD found in Iraq." I saw only a handful of headlines which read similarly to, "No WMD found in Iraq thus far." Instead, the liberal-controlled media clearly tried to portray this as a failure for Bush (much like they did with his address to the United Nations in September, 2003). Here are just a handful of the headlines used to cover Kay's report:

* "Inspectors Find Aims, Not Arms; Interim report appears to undermine prewar White House and CIA claims about Iraq. Hussein may have hoped to acquire the weapons."—the *Los Angeles Times*, **October 3, 2003.**

(Did they read the same interim report that I did?)

* "Major Finds Unlikely in Iraq Report; The CIA's chief weapons hunter is to deliver data to Congress next week,

but it remains unclear how much, if any, will be made public."—the *Los Angeles Times*, **September 25, 2003.**
(Well, that's the key isn't it? The public will not be privileged to top secret information until it is SAFE to be revealed.)

* "U.S. REPORT FINDS NO ILLICIT ARMS."
—the *Boston Globe*, **October 3, 2003.**
(They failed to use the terms "thus far.")

* "THE STRUGGLE FOR IRAQ: THE SEARCH; No Illicit Arms Found in Iraq, U.S. Inspector Tells Congress."—the *New York Times*, **(www.nytimes.com) October 3, 2003.**
(I didn't know the postwar in Iraq was a struggle, but now I do.)

* "THE STRUGGLE FOR IRAQ: ASSESSMENT; A Reckoning: Iraq Arms Report Poses Test for Bush."
—the *New York Times*, **(www.nytimes.com) October 3, 2003.**
(Is this what the War on Iraq is all about—a test for Bush?)

* "David Kay: Little evidence of Iraq WMD weapons."
—*MSNBC*, **October 2, 2003.**
(Obviously, Kay must have had a separate report.)

Reports of Mass Deception

* "No WMD found in Iraq." *—AOL News,* **October 3, 2003.**
*(Again, the terms "thus far" would paint a different
and more accurate perspective.)*

First of all, the investigation is young; it's not even
halfway done. Kay said that the current discoveries were
interim, and it's too soon in the 90-day-old investigation
to conclude that there are no WMD in Iraq. Secondly, it
is just an update, not the final report. Thirdly, you would
think that the great discoveries made *thus far* in the
investigation would be enough for the War on Iraq
skeptics. Let's take a look at these discoveries:[13]

* A clandestine network of laboratories and safehouses
within the Iraqi Intelligence Service that contained
equipment suitable for research in the production of
chemical and biological weapons. This kind of equipment
was explicitly mentioned in Hans Blix's requests for
information, but was instead concealed from Blix
throughout his investigations.
*(Ah, but Saddam was only trying to hide this because
he was trying not to be misunderstood. After all,
attacks like the ones on 9/11 are planned in terms of
honesty.)*

* A prison laboratory complex, which may have been
used in human testing of biological weapons agents. Iraqi

officials working to prepare for United Nations inspections in 2002 and 2003 were explicitly ordered not to acknowledge the existence of the prison complex.
(There is a simple explanation for this— those complexes are sacred, like tombs—"shhh.")

* So-called "reference strains" of biological organisms, which can be used to produce biological weapons. The strains were found in a scientist's home.
(Coincidence! Bush planted this for sure!)

* New research on agents applicable to biological weapons, including Congo Crimean Hemorrhagic Fever, and continuing research on ricin and aflatoxin—all of which was, again, concealed from Hans Blix despite his specific request for any such information.
(This is a lie! It is nothing more than a feeble attempt to discredit Saddam's effort for designing a formula to heal cancer.)

* Plans and advanced design work on new long-range missiles with ranges up to at least 1,000 kilometers— well beyond the 150-kilometer limit imposed on Iraq by the United Nations Security Council. These missiles would have allowed Saddam to threaten targets from Ankara to Cairo.
(Who cares—not our problem, right?)

Reports of Mass Deception

* Evidences of efforts to destroy WMD programs, including sabotaged computer hard drives in government buildings and burned and shredded documents. *(Again, Baath Party loyalists do not want Bush to get the historical credit for unveiling the cure for cancer.)*

Regarding these discoveries, National Security Adviser Condoleezza Rice said, "Had any one of these examples been discovered last winter, the Security Council would have had to meet, and I believe that they would have had no choice but to take exactly the course that President Bush followed." [14]

Robert Kagan and William Kristol pointed out in an article in the October 20, 2003 issue of the *Weekly Standard* that an Iraqi citizen led coalition forces to a number of hidden MiG fighter jets beneath the ground. They were making the argument that U.S. soldiers did not make the discovery on their own and that locating WMD in Iraq will be a far greater challenge due to the 130 ammunition depots dispersed throughout the 169,000-square-mile country. The article highlighted that United Nations inspectors discovered, under Saddam's regime, that the Iraqi military stored chemical weaponry at those same ammunition areas and only 10 of the 130 had been inspected thus far at the time of the article.[15]

Why don't we hear about these facts and discoveries in the mainstream news media? How many times, or even have you, heard about the aforementioned evidence on the news? How often do you read about the positives in David Kay's investigation in newspaper outlets? Just like you rarely hear any coverage regarding anything positive in postwar Iraq, the same goes for the positives concerning the WMD investigation in Iraq. Why is this? Because the liberal-controlled news media's objective is to discredit the Bush administration and anything regarding conservative progress. Their agenda is to portray an illusion of domestic and international crisis for the sake of partisan left-wing gain, ratings and viewer interest at the expense of reporting fair, balanced and accurate news.

Still, even with all the prewar proof of Iraq's chemical and biological weapons programs by dozens of intelligence agencies, including the United Nations' own intelligence, this altogether is not enough.

The extreme anti-war skeptics are perhaps unknowingly labeling themselves as a gullible group that believes Saddam had no WMD and no current ambitions or secret plans to use them against Americans, either by himself or by selling them to terrorists. They are seemingly abandoning the fact that somehow after 12 years and 16 United Nations resolutions, Saddam wasn't trying to hide something from the rest of the world. They appear to forget the fact that Saddam used chemical weapons before by alluding to the notion that perhaps he wouldn't do such an act of inhumanity again, and the War on Iraq was jumping the gun to a tune of a false sense of risk to national security. More and more, they are sounding just like Saddam with questions such as, "What weapons of mass destruction?" Their argument continually points out that they would have preferred for Bush to have waited for more concrete proof of Saddam's WMD and his supposed threat to our nation.

Would another 9/11 with biological weaponry have sufficed?

"We don't want the smoking gun to be a mushroom cloud." **—Condoleeza Rice, U.S. National Security Advisor.**[16]

CHAPTER 6
The Ties that Bind

Reports of Mass Deception

Is it that hard to believe that Saddam Hussein had ties to Osama bin Laden's al-Qaeda network? Recent discoveries from amongst the rubble in the aftermath of the War on Iraq indicate that the skeptics of such an alliance were wrong to doubt a possible connection. Accusations of such an association are looked upon as elaborate far-out spins designed by conservatives to fool Americans into further support of the War on Iraq.

It has been long alleged by United States intelligence sources, and more recently by the Bush administration, that there are ties between Saddam Hussein's regime and Osama bin Laden's al-Qaeda network.

"There are al-Qaeda in a number of locations in Iraq. In a vicious, repressive dictatorship that exercises near total control over its population, it's very hard to imagine that the government is not aware of what is taking place in the country."—**U.S. Defense Secretary Donald Rumsfeld in August, 2002.**[1]

"Saddam Hussein aids and protects terrorists, including members of al-Qaeda." —**President George W. Bush, January, 2003.**[2]

"We know members of both organizations have met at least eight times at very senior levels since the early 1990s. In 1996 . . . bin Laden met with a senior Iraqi intelligence official in Khartoum, and later met with the director of the Iraqi intelligence service."—**Secretary of State Colin Powell.**[3]

Why would they think this? Did they just conjure up that theory based on a hypnotizing foreplay of political spin, with *no* intelligence evidence whatsoever and solely designed to make Bush look justified with the War on Iraq? No! They believe that the intelligence they have clearly proves a connection between al-Qaeda and Iraq. However, no evidence they have proves that Saddam, or any member of his regime, had any part whatsoever in the plot of the 9/11 attacks. Liberals continue to berate us with this fact, as if this somehow vindicates their notion that adding al-Qaeda and Iraqi ties to the list of reasons to go to war with Iraq was a political ploy designed by the Bush administration to win support. The problem with that theory is the Bush administration already had the majority of American support along with a vast collective support among other nations.

The skeptics of such an alliance have this one valid argument of contention: there is no concrete evidence linking Saddam directly to the 9/11 plot. The key word here is "plot," because there is ample evidence of tying various contacts between Iraq and al-Qaeda.

But isn't the mere fact that senior members of the fallen Iraqi regime had contact with al-Qaeda, for

Reports of Mass Deception

whatever reason, justification enough? Isn't the War on Iraq part of the grand plan for the War on Terrorism, and didn't President Bush say that countries who harbor or lend support to terrorists are now targets in the War on Terrorism?

It is recorded by intelligence sources that Iraq has met, harbored, and supported terrorist groups including al-Qaeda. During Secretary of State Colin Powell's remarks to the United Nations Security Council on February 5, 2003, he shared, in further detail, some of the uncorroborated (*Ah, these are the real reports of mass deception! Only when Saddam signs-off on them will they be corroborated. Mr. Powell, have you gone mad?*) reports on Iraq and al-Qaeda links received by the U.S. that CIA Director George Tenet announced back in October of 2002. They are as follows:[4]

1. Iraq harbored a terrorist network headed by Abu Musab al-Zarqawi, an associate and collaborator of Osama bin Laden and his al-Qaeda lieutenants, who oversaw a terrorist training camp in Afghanistan. When the U.S. ousted the Taliban during Operation Enduring Freedom, this camp relocated to northeastern Iraq where Ansar al-Islam, a senior Saddam regime official, granted safe haven to al-Zarqawi. "He (Zarqawi) also traveled to Baghdad in May of 2002 for medical treatment, staying in the capital of Iraq for two months."

2. Iraqi officials and al-Qaeda members met 8 times since the early 1990's "at very senior levels."

3. "A senior defector, one of Saddam's former intelligence chiefs in Europe, says Saddam sent his agents to Afghanistan, sometime in the mid-1990s, to provide training to al-Qaeda members on document forgery."

4. "From the late 1990's until 2001, the Iraqi Embassy in Pakistan played the role of liaison to the al-Qaeda organization."

Another fact that clearly shows the "heart" of Saddam's regime was how they responded to the 9/11 attacks on America. Iraq was the only Arab-Muslim country that praised the 9/11 attacks, expressing sympathy for Osama bin Laden and saying on the record that the U.S. is "...reaping the fruits of [its] crimes against humanity."[5] That certainly doesn't prove anything. However, as the saying goes, "Birds of a feather, flock together!"

To discredit the Bush administration's claims of an al-Qaeda and Iraq connection, the liberal-controlled mainstream media, accompanied by liberal extremists' solo acts, went spinning conspiracy theories like clothes dryers on crack. They told the tale of vast allegations suggesting that the intelligence that Colin Powell was

Reports of Mass Deception

sharing to the United Nations was weak at best.

"One of the things that concerns me is the continued reference to the war in Iraq as part of the War on Terrorism. There's not much evidence to support that linkage," said Sen. Bob Graham of Florida, the top Democrat on the Senate Intelligence Committee and a former presidential candidate.[6]

"There was no significant pattern of cooperation between Iraq and the al-Qaeda terrorist operation," former State Department intelligence official Greg Thielmann said.[7]

"The relationships that were plotted were episodic, not continuous," a former Bush administration intelligence official said.[8]

Notice the key words here— "Not much," "no significant pattern," and "episodic." They had to use these terms because they cannot dispute the fact that the evidence recorded by the CIA and shared by Colin Powell is real! They are documented! There is no disputing that!

The various arguments suggesting that the Bush administration conjured up false theories designed to portray an al-Qaeda and Iraq connection is a clear example of how some of these liberal extremists have taken on the role of Saddam Hussein's defense team. This in turn forsakes the crucial current crises of terrorism and creates distrust and lack of faith in the Bush administration.

Whether or not you believe that the evidence the CIA has on Iraq and al-Qaeda is weak or strong, the connection between Saddam and bin Laden is now becoming more and more evident everyday. On April 26, 2003, documents found in the bombed headquarters of the Mukhabaret, Iraq's intelligence service, revealed that an al-Qaeda envoy was invited clandestinely to Baghdad in March 1998, according to Britain's *Telegraph*. The papers show that the purpose of the meeting was to establish a relationship between Iraq and al-Qaeda based on their mutual hatred for America. It also spelled out the objective to establish secure methods for the Iraqi regime to make contact with Osama bin Laden. Ironically, the meeting took place just 5 months prior to the al-Qaeda bombing of two U.S. embassies in east Africa, killing 80 on August 8, 1998.[9]

During the War on Iraq, the discovery of terrorist camps by U.S. and coalition forces further supported the evidences already recorded that Saddam's regime supported, financed, and harbored other terrorist organizations besides al-Qaeda. In an article published by Britain's *Telegraph* on April 17, 2003, documents were discovered in an Iraqi spies' Baghdad headquarters that show "Iraq's charge d'affaires in Nairobi, Fallah Hassan Al Rubdie, was in discussion with the Allied Democratic

Reports of Mass Deception

Forces, an Ugandan guerrilla group with ties to other anti-western Islamist organizations."[10]

Which ever way you spin it, Saddam Hussein was an ally to terrorism and a source for terrorists. Osama bin Laden may have labeled Saddam an "infidel," but he has also said that he could work with anyone who was an enemy of the United States. After the brutal attacks of 9/11, how long could America have waited before dealing with the imminent threat that the Iraqi regime posed? If we had given weapons inspectors more time, if we had waited for France, Germany, and Russia to jump on board, and if we had continued to try to negotiate with Saddam Hussein, how long would it have been until an act of terror, far worse that 9/11, crept upon our shores? It is one thing to turn the other cheek and try to reason with our enemies; however, just as when you are dealing with termites – there is no reasoning, no bargaining, no hope for change. They will tear down your house, unless you fight back!

CHAPTER 7
Parallel Delusions

Reports of Mass Deception

In an attempt to accent their negative War on Iraq propaganda with other delusions of Bush-failing falsities, the liberal extremists, like Spiderman, continue to spin massive webs throughout our society, painting an illusion of something that is fictional, just as Spiderman is. However, that is where the similarities end! Spiderman spins a web of triumph, optimism and truth, whereas the extreme left-wing's web is one containing portions of a truth, woven into a deception designed to make Bush look pathetic. Just as the Spiderman comics, cartoons and movies are quite entertaining, the fiction-based facts coming forth from some of the mainstream news media outlets are so far from reality, one can get a better picture of current events from the Sunday comics. As major combat operations in Iraq were subsiding, the partisan attacks against the Bush administration's handling of the war were just beginning. However, criticism regarding the War on Iraq was only part of the rhetoric.

When the $350 billion tax package was signed into law by President Bush on May 28, 2003, after the bill was passed by the House of Representatives 231-230 and the Senate 51-50 on Friday, May 23, 2003, the leftists flocked to dissolve its merits and benefits like ants on a grilled chicken sandwich. The tax cut was the third largest in U.S. history and immediately presented viable solutions that could help boost the economy across the board with the following benefits:

* Small businesses can now write off $100,000 in new equipment purchases.

* All businesses will be able to expense half their investments this year (2003).

* Personal tax cuts are retroactive to Jan. 1, so employees will see larger paychecks in the second half of 2003.

* Many parents will get an advance refund on their tax return worth as much as $400 per child in 2003.

* Married couples will have a lessened marriage penalty for filing together.

* Investors will keep more of their earned money with rates on dividends and capital gains dipping to 15%.

* $20 billion in aid to states.

"By leaving American families with more to spend, more to save and more to invest, these reforms will help boost the nation's economy and create jobs," said President Bush during his radio address, May 17, 2003.[1]

Reports of Mass Deception

Despite the benefits of the new tax rates, anti-Bush advocates had to spin a negative web around something that is, without a doubt, partly responsible for putting a sinking economy not only currently above water, but on a path to a slow but steady recovery powered by a Bush administration goal of generating 1 million new jobs by the end of 2004.[2]

Just shortly over a month after the tax cut was signed into law, its effects on our economy were becoming evident. Disposable incomes went up 1.5 percent which, in turn, elevated consumer purchasing 0.8 percent partially due to the $100 billion in tax rebate checks sent back to families with children, according to the Commerce Department.[3]

In September 2003, 88,000 new jobs were created from office-related to blue-collar-related work, despite a loss of 31,000 mining and manufacturing-related jobs, according to the Labor Department. The 57,000 new jobs are said to possibly be a major part of why the economy is showing signs of recovery, especially since it came after eight months of continuous job losses. The unemployment rate in the U.S. subsequently fell to 6.1% in September 2003.[4]

"The consensus of economists was that the plan needed to be responsible, immediate and tailored to create the most jobs for the money. Unfortunately, the plan the

President signed today missed on all three," said Senate Minority Leader Tom Daschle.[5]

Would Democrats have been more happy with a $350 billion tax hike?

Liberals jumped all over this tax cut with the argument that working families on the edge of poverty, would not benefit from this tax cut. They were implying that Bush did not included the poor people, arguing that 82.9% of all households will receive less than the average benefit projected by the Bush administration and 53.4% would receive $100 or less while a majority would receive no benefit at all, according to the Center on Budget and Policy Priorities, a nonpartisan think tank.[6]

The Democrats were lobbying for *no* tax cut at all as Vice-President Dick Cheney broke a 50-50 tie in the Senate to enable this bill to be signed by the President. Democrats were not only collectively against this tax cut, but collectively squabbled over the initial $726 billion proposed by Bush in the first place, thus forcing him to settle for only $350 billion in tax relief. It appears that the Democrats were the ones desiring to keep more of Americans hard-earned money in the government's pockets!

"Why are they for a little-bitty tax-relief package?" said President Bush of senators opposing the initial $726 billion.[7]

Reports of Mass Deception

The consensus among liberals was that only a few wealthy friends benefit from this tax cut. Interesting. I benefit from this tax rate cut, and I can assure you that I am not wealthy, nor a friend of Bush. I'm just a middle-class average "Joe" with a wife and three toddlers trying to make his way in the universe. But, is this about a tax rate cut or about feeding the non-taxpayer and homeless? Last I checked, the two issues are separate. Every taxpayer will benefit from this $350 billion tax cut if he is employed, paying taxes and has children. It is correct that if you are making less, claim less or not working at all, that you will not receive the same exact benefit amounts as the family who made more, claimed more or actually worked.

As for the tax cut not benefiting those on welfare and those out of work with children, what does this tax cut have to do with that issue? It's not that they don't matter; it's just a separate issue altogether. Besides, how can a non-taxpayer benefit from a tax rate cut anyway? Better yet, why should he? And mind you, I am not talking about those on unemployment! Bush helped those individuals out immensely on the same day by also signing legislation extending federal unemployment benefits through December 2003, for those who can work and want to work, but are out of a job and/or can't get employed due to the nature of current economic times. How many millions does that benefit? Nearly 9 million people are currently out of a job. Obviously, Bush has not overlooked them with this extension.

The Internal Revenue Service put new tax tables on its web site so employers could reduce the amount of federal income tax withheld from workers' paychecks as the tax cut bill prescribed. Employers were told to use the new tables making it possible for some employees to see larger checks shortly after the bill was signed. How many millions does that benefit? Mind you, this is *everyone* who earns a legal paycheck!

Starting in the last week of July 2003, the government began sending checks to the 25 million parents who claimed a 2002 child tax credit. The automatic refunds—no phone calls or forms required–will be advance payments on their 2003 credits, in an amount equal to the increase provided by the new law up to $400 per child. I am one of those 25 million that benefited from this, and quite frankly, I am not rich and I can use it!

> "By leaving American families with more to spend, more to save and more to invest, these reforms will help boost the nation's economy and create jobs," President Bush said during his May 24, 2003 radio address. "When people have extra take-home pay, there's greater demand for goods and services. And employers will need more workers to meet that demand."[8]

Reports of Mass Deception

Desperately attempting to find something to hang Bush on, liberal extremists soon realized that the tax rate cut was smiled upon by a greater majority of Americans because it puts more cash in their pockets. Consequently, they went on to the next item on Bush's list – Medicare!

The House and Senate approved differing legislation regarding an increase of prescription drug coverage to the government's health plan, Medicare. Spawned by Bush's original Medicare proposal, which would offer the first subsidies to the health plan's 38-year history, the differing legislations are essentially two revamped versions of Bush's original proposal with some subtle, and not so subtle, differences in each. The task at hand now for the two houses is to reach a compromise that would be acceptable to a majority of the lawmakers in each chamber. To make a long story short, Bush has pushed for a better, more comprehensive prescription drug program for seniors - a program for which seniors have been crying out for years.

> "Today, doctors routinely treat their patients with prescription drugs, preventive care and groundbreaking medical devices, but Medicare coverage has not kept pace with these changes," said President Bush on June, 7, 2003 during his weekly radio address. "Our goal is to give seniors the best, most innovative care."[9]

Bush explained that seniors who want to stay in the current Medicare system will have that option with a new prescription drug benefit. He said that seniors who want enhanced benefits, such as coverage for preventive care and a cap on out-of-pocket expenses, will have that choice, as well.

However, for some Democrats, that isn't good enough. First, some say that Bush has pushed this Medicare proposal solely for the reason of taking the issue out of the Democratic Party's hands. Medicare reform has been a driving issue for many Democratic campaigns, and by Bush showing interest in this typically Democratic-pushed issue, he gains support from seniors for the next presidential election. Personally, I'd like to believe he created this proposal because he recognized the need for a better Medicare program. Presidents of the United States have been known to lobby for reform because of a genuine conviction.

Even more amusing is the notion that Bush's plan *invades* seniors' privacy. Supposedly, under one version of the proposal, the health insurance industry would have access to the income data of every senior citizen in America, because it would need that information for seniors to have the privilege of choosing different types of programs within this new system. Does anyone really have privacy anymore? You can't even buy a refrigerator on credit at a department store without giving out your

Reports of Mass Deception

Social Security number. You certainly can't qualify for any financial aid, be it for medical insurance or whatever, without disclosing basic financial information, such as household income to determine if you qualify for aid and at what level. It's not as if they're going to ask how many freckles you have on your right leg—now that's private!

However, Bush's adversaries regarding this $400 billion Medicare-reform package include some conservative skeptics as well. It has been said of Bush, when he was governor of Texas, that he was very good at working with issues of concern from both Democratic and Republican parties. Medicare is usually an issue taken up by the Democrats. However, Bush saw the viable problems over the current Medicare system, and he felt it was in the best interest of Americans to revamp the system to better suit today's situations.

Despite grumblings on both sides, the House's Medicare bill was passed 216-215 while the Senate's bill was passed 76-21 on June 27, 2003. The President told both the House and Senate to resolve their differences sooner than later so that a final bill can be placed on his desk for him to sign, giving seniors prescription drug coverage for the first time ever under Medicare.

It does seem that Bush has been pushing all the right political buttons lately. It's almost to the point where it can be perceived it's being done to undermine those who obsessively oppose him. You can tell someone is doing a decent job when the complaints about his efforts are based on far-out spin. However, when you practice truthful politics, and base legislative decisions for the country on the sole purpose of bettering the nation and preserving freedom — rather than for partisan gain – pushing the right buttons just comes *naturally*. Bush's tackling of prescription drug and Medicare issues and actually *doing* something about it will *undoubtedly* become a major blow to the Democratic Party by removing that issue from their arsenal of debate. However, the new Medicare bill, whatever its final version turns out to be, will also *undoubtedly* create new partisan rhetoric, *naturally*.

Naturally, there are many issues that need to be dealt with in our society. However, each issue is separate from the other and the current administration seems to have balanced it all very responsibly. The Bush administration has handled the economic mess handed to them from the prior administration with flying colors as we never really entered the true recession we were slated for. The Bush administration has handled the attacks on our country and terrorism with a firm, swift hand, and there hasn't been a terrorist attack in our country since September 11, 2001. It has now made moves to catapult the economy back into the positive. President Bush has taken a look at the Medicare issues, and instead of just talking reform, actually started reform! Finally, Bush has kept his word to the American people and has, as promised, dealt with

Reports of Mass Deception

Iraq and other countries harboring and supporting terrorist organizations swiftly and effectively. He did not just "talk-the-talk" after the events of September 11, 2001 to casually console the American people into a false sense of stability and justice. He meant it when he said that terrorists would be hunted down and brought to justice as well as the governments and regimes of nations which support and harbor them. Whether you agree with Bush or not, he is a leader who says what he means and follows through with his promises. Americans have come to respect that about him. That very significant character trait may become the deciding factor in the 2004 Presidential election. For those who think they can do a better job than he has during this time of overwhelming historical crisis, you're also probably one of those people who think you can throw a pass better than Pittsburgh Steelers quarterback Tommy Maddox. Maybe you can, but it's much easier done on your "X-Box" game system than out there live on the field of play!

God bless America, and our troops!

NOTES:

CHAPTER ONE. The Shroud of Illusion

1. Frank Newport and Joseph Carrol, "Are the News Media Too Liberal? Forty-five percent of Americans say yes," Gallup News Service, October 8, 2003.

2. "National Survey of the Role of Polls in Policymaking," Kaiser Family Foundation, a project by Princeton Survey Research Associates in conjunction with Public Perspective, a magazine published by the Roper Center for Public Opinion Research in 2001.

3. "Editors Realize Liberal Slant," *Editor & Publisher* magazine, January 17, 1998 and *Media Watch,* www.mediaresearch.org, February 1998.

4. "Anti-war grumps, whiners, et cetera," *Washington Times*, Section: OPED, P. A21, April 14, 2003.

5. Ibid.

6. Ibid.

7. Ibid.

8. Ibid.

9. Ibid.

10. "Saddam killed Missile Chief to Thwart U.N. Team," *Telegraph* (Britain), February 2, 2003.

11. "Iraq: the threat of war- a letter to British Prime Minister, Tony Blair from 'Iraqi Exiles in UK,'" www.caabu.org (CAABU Campaigns Section), February 15, 2003.

12. "Eight European leaders are as One with President Bush," *Wall Street Journal*, January 30, 2003.

13. "East European Nations Back U.S. on Iraq," *Guardian Unlimited* (www.guardian.co.uk), February 2003.

14. "U.S. to have access to 21 countries in Iraq War: Armitage," *Palestine Chronicle*, January 31, 2003.

15. "Experts: Iraq has tons of chemical weapons," CNN, September 4, 2002.

16. "UN inspectors uncover proof of Saddam's nuclear bomb plans," *Telegraph* (Britain), January 19, 2003.

17. "Saddam Killed Abu Nidal over al-Qaeda row," *Telegraph* (Britain), August, 25, 2002.

18. "Iraq's Tie to Al-Qaeda Terrorists, Airline Hijackings," www.rushlimbaugh.com, "Satellite Photos Believed To Show Airliner for Training Hijackers from Aviation Week and Space Technology," January 7, 2002.

19. "The Sabah Khodada (former Iraqi captain) Interview in which he speaks of a terrorist training camp in Iraq," PBS-Frontline:gunning for Saddam, www.pbs.org.

20. "Iraq Nukes Sites Up and Atom Again," *New York Post*, September 7, 2002.

21. "Exiles' 'liberate Iraq' plea," BBC News Online, February 22, 2003.

22. "Iraq exiles back Blair's stance," BBC News Online, February 18, 2003.

23. "Saddam killed missile chief to thwart UN Team," *Telegraph* (Britain), February 2, 2003.

24. "BBC chief attacks U.S. media war coverage," *ABC Newsline*,

Australia, (www.abc.net.au), April 25, 2003.

25. Tom Barrett, "Marines Watch FOX TV," *Conservative Truth*, www.conservativetruth.org, March 24, 2003.

CHAPTER TWO. Rally the Troops

1. Dana Blanton, "Poll: Public Unites Behind War," *FOX News*, www.foxnews.com, April 10, 2003.

2. "Few Students Protesting War," *Young America's Foundation*, www.yaf.org, March 20, 2003.

3. "Rush's Stack of Saddam Stuff," www.rushlimbaugh.com.

4. "Democrats rally behind U.S. troops," *Washington Times*, March 18, 2003.

5. Ibid.

6. Ibid.

7. Dana Blanton, "Poll: Public Unites Behind War," *FOX News Channel*, www.foxnews.com, April 10, 2003.

8. "Democrats rally behind U.S. troops," *Washington Times*, March 18, 2003.

9. Henry Lamb, "The Charter for Global Democracy," *American Policy Center*, www.americanpolicy.org, " The UN's Millennium Threat To Liberty."

CHAPTER THREE. The War on Iraq

1. "Faces of War," www.softsynth.com/faces.

2. Associated Press, AOL News, April 10, 2003.

3. Ellen Knickmeyer and David Crary, *Washington Post*, April 10, 2003.

4. Associated Press, *Fox News Channel*, April 10, 2003.

5. Associated Press, "Marines Help Topple Statue; Baghdadis Loot City," *Fox News Channel*, April 10, 2003.

6. "Iraqis Celebrate As U.S. Takes Baghdad," *Washington Times*, April 10, 2003.

7. "U.S. hails end of Saddam era: Statue toppled in central Baghdad; Crowds cheer U.S. marines; Forces focus on Tikrit," *Guardian Unlimited* (www.guardian.co.uk), April 9, 2003.

8. *The Rush Limbaugh Show*, April 10, 2003.

9. Truth Detector, www.rushlimbaugh.com, April 10, 2003.

10. "Anti-war grumps, whiners, et cetera," *Washington Times*, Section: OPED, P. A21, April 14, 2003.

CHAPTER FOUR. The Bleak Postwar

1. Jim Abrams, Associated Press, www.yahoo.com, April 17, 2003.

2. Stephen Dinan and Amy Fagan, *Washington Times*, April 11, 2003.

3. Ann Coulter, *Treason*, New York: Crown Forum, 2003, p.20.

4. Ann Coulter, "No Quagmire Here!" www.anncoulter.com, September 3, 2003.

5. "Democratic hopefuls blast Bush," CNN.com, "Inside Politics, February 23, 2003.

6. Ibid.

7. Fred Barnes, "Hillary Gets Tough," *Weekly Standard*, September 24, 2003.

8. Ibid.

9. "Bush UN speech persuades few: World leaders, Democrats

deride President's address as too little, too late," MSNBC, September 23, 2003.

10. "Under fire at UN, Bush rejects early Iraq transfer," Reuters, September 23, 2003.

11. "U.S. slammed for bypassing UN over Iraq," *Dawn* (Pakistan English newspaper), September 23, 2003.

12. "President Bush Addresses United Nations General Assembly," www.whitehouse.gov, September 23, 2003.

13. Stephen Schwartz, "As it was in Kosovo, the 'international community' is a threat to postwar Iraq," *Weekly Standard*, April 14, 2003, Volume 008, Issue 30.

14. Jennifer Harper, "The first rigorous and scientifically conducted sampling of public sentiment in Iraq," "Majority in Baghdad say war worth it," *Washington Times*, September 25, 2003.

15. Ibid.

16. Ibid.

17. "American Resolve Critical in Iraq, Says Representative Jim Marshall," *Washington Times*, October 1, 2003.

18. Ibid.

19. "Ask the White House," www.whitehouse.gov/ask, October 9, 2003.

20. Ibid.

21. Charles J. Hanley, "Ramadan Begins With Bloodbath in Baghdad." Associated Press, *AOL News*, Web id=20031026060809990001, October 27, 2003.

22. "Baghdad Blasts Kill at Least 35," *FOX News Channel*, www.foxnews.com, October 27, 2003.

23. Alissa J. Rubin, David Lamb and James Gerstenzang, "Baghdad Rocked by Bombs; Dozens Dead," *Los Angeles Times*, October 27, 2003.

24. "Under Fire" and "The Battle at Home," AOL News, "The Daily Pulse," Web id=20031027105109990001, October 27, 2003.

25. Stephen F. Hayes, "Distinguishing foe from foe," *Weekly Standard*, November 10, 2003, Volume 009, Issue 09.

26. Tini Tran, "A Tragic Day for America," Associated Press, AOL News, Web id=20031102061509990001, November 2, 2003.

27. Stephen F. Hayes, "Distinguishing foe from foe," *Weekly Standard*, November 10, 2003, Volume 009, Issue 09.

CHAPTER 5. I Want My WMD

1. Henry Lamb, "The Charter for Global Democracy," American Policy Center, (www.americanpolicy.org).

2. Bill Sammon, "Cheney says U.S. can wage war without global OK," *Washington Times*, October 10, 2003.

3. Bill Sammon, "Bush hails 6 months after Saddam," *Washington Times*, October 9, 2003.

4. Robert Kagan & William Kristol, "Why We Went to War," "The case for the war in Iraq, with testimony from Bill Clinton," *Weekly Standard*, October 20, 2003, Volume 009, Issue 06.

5. "The Decision to go to War in Iraq: Ninth Report of Session," House of Commons Foreign Affairs Committee, 2002-2003, Volume I, page 16.

6. "The Decision to go to War in Iraq: Ninth Report of Session," House of Commons Foreign Affairs Committee, 2002-2003,

Reports of Mass Deception

Volume I, page 9.

7. "International Special Report: Iraq," *Washington Post*, (www.washingtonpost.com/wp-srv/inatl/longterm/iraq/maps/satindex.htm).

8. "International Special Report: Iraq," *Washington Post*, (http://www.washingtonpost.com/wp-srv/inatl/longterm/iraq/stories/graphic022298.htm).

9. "Letter by Eight European leaders in support of the United States," Rush's Stack of Saddam Stuff, www.rushlimbaugh.com.

10. Ibid.

11. Ibid.

12. "Evidence of arms 'intent' found," *Washington Times*, October 3, 2003.

13. "Evidence of Iraqi weapons programs disclosed by CIA weapons inspector David Kay," CNN.com, "Inside Politics," October 2, 2003.

14. Bill Sammon, "Rice says report on Saddam validates move to wage war," *Washington Times*, October 9, 2003.

15. Robert Kagan & William Kristol, "Why We Went to War," "The case for the war in Iraq, with testimony from Bill Clinton," *Weekly Standard*, October 20, 2003, Volume 009, Issue 06.

16. *CNN Late Edition*, September 8, 2002.

Chapter 6. The Ties that Bind

1. Con Coughlin, "Saddam killed Abu Nidal over al-Qaeda row," *Telegraph* (Britain), August 25, 2002.

2. "State of the Union Address," www.whitehouse.gov, January

2003.

3. Con Coughlin, "Bush always suspected Saddam was behind 9/11," *Telegraph* (Britain), April 27, 2003.

4. "Remarks to the UN Security Council," U.S. Department of State, (www.state.gov), February 5, 2003.

5. "Patterns of Global Terrorism, Released by the Office of the Coordinator for Counterterrorism," U.S. Department of State, (www.state.gov), May 21, 2002.

6. Associated Press, "Bush overstated Iraq links to al-Qaeda, former intelligence officials say," *USA Today*, July 13, 2003.

7. Ibid.

8. Ibid.

9. Inigo Gilmore, "The proof that Saddam worked with bin Laden," *Telegraph* (Britain)," April 27, 2003.

10. Philip Smucker and Adrian Blomfield, "Saddam link to terror group," *Telegraph* (Britain), April 17, 2003.

CHAPTER 7. Parallel Delusions

1. Associated Press, "Bush defends tax-cut package, says it will kick-start economy," *Washington Times*, May 25, 2003.

2. Patrice Hill, "Job gains halt long losing streak," *Washington Times*, October 4, 2003.

3. Patrice Hill, "Tax rebates prompted July consumer shopping spree," *Washington Times*, August 30, 2003.

4. Patrice Hill, "Job gains halt long losing streak," *Washington Times*, October 4, 2003.

5. Stephen Dinan, "Bush signs his 2nd big tax cut," *Washington*

Reports of Mass Deception

Times, May 29, 2003.

6. Andrew Lee and Joel Friedman, "Administration Continues to Rely on Misleading Use of 'Averages' to Describe Tax-Cut Benefits," *Center on Budget and Policy Priorities*, www.cbpp.org, May 28, 2003.

7. Associated Press, "Bush defends tax-cut package, says it will kick-start economy," *Washington Times*, May 25, 2003.

8. Ibid.

9. Associated Press, "Bush outlines proposals for Medicare," *Washington Times*, June 8, 2003.

INDEX

Peter Chase

Reports of Mass Deception

ABOUT THE AUTHOR

Peter Chase *has been a practicing journalist & copy editor since 1990. He is currently the editor-in-chief of the* **Monthly Post** *(www.themonthlypost.com), a free community-oriented magazine in southwestern Allegheny County in western Pennsylvania.*

The **Monthly Post** *is one of the largest monthly publications in the greater Pittsburgh area, with an estimated readership of 55,000 per issue. Mr. Chase has a degree in journalism and is a graduate of the Connecticut School of Broadcasting.*